**Books are to be returned on or before
the last date below.**

5 JUN 2009
2 3 OCT 2015

LIBREX —

CLASSIFYING ANIMALS

Birds

Sarah Wilkes

HODDER
Wayland

An imprint of Hodder Children's Books

CLASSIFYING ANIMALS

Titles in this series:

Amphibians Birds Fish Insects Mammals Reptiles

For more information on this series and other Hodder Wayland titles, go to www.hodderwayland.co.uk

Conceived and produced for Hodder Wayland by

Nutshell
MEDIA

Intergen House, 65–67 Western Road, Hove BN3 2JQ, UK
www.nutshellmedialtd.co.uk

Consultant: Jane Mainwaring, Natural History Museum
Editor: Polly Goodman
Designer: Tim Mayer
Picture research: Morgan Interactive Ltd and Victoria Coombs

Published in Great Britain in 2005 by Hodder Wayland, an imprint of Hodder Children's Books.
© Copyright 2005 Hodder Wayland

British Library Cataloguing in Publication Data
Wilkes, Sarah, 1964–
Birds. – (Classifying animals)
1. Birds – Classification – Juvenile literature
I. Title
598'.012

ISBN 0 7502 4751 7

Cover photographs: the eyes of a Cape Eagle owl.
Title page (clockwise from top left): a pheasant, a peacock, a kingfisher and a penguin chick.
Chapter openers: close-up photographs of the feathers of (from top to bottom) a blue tit, a pheasant, a peacock fan, a flamingo and a peacock (single feather).

Picture acknowledgements
Corbis *cover*; **Ecoscene** 4 (Fritz Polking), 7 (John Farmer), 9 (Graham Neden), 13 (Fritz Polking), 14 (Peter Cairns), 18, 19, 20 (Fritz Polking), 24, 25 (Frank Blackburn), 33 (Michael Gore), 35, 37, 40 (Fritz Polking), 42 (Martin Beames); **naturepl.com** 5 (Dave Watts), 6 (Tony Herald), 8 (Pete Oxford), 10 (Peter Scoones), 11 (Tony Heald), 12 (Terry Andrewartha), 15 (John Cancalosi), 16 (John Downer), 17 (Solvin Zanki), 21, 22 (Mike Wilkes), 23 (Brian Lightfoot), 26 (Bengt Lundberg), 27 (David Pike), 28 (Bernard Castelein), 29 (Hans Christoph Kappel), 30 (Niall Benvie), 31 (Lynn M. Stone), 32 (Mike Wilkes), 34 (Richard Du Toit), 36 (Mike Wilkes), 39 (Phil Savoie), 41 (Dave Watts), 43 (Mark Payne-Gill); **nhpa** 38 (Mike Lane)

Printed and bound in China.

Hodder Children's Books
A division of Hodder Headline Limited
338 Euston Road, London NW1 3BH

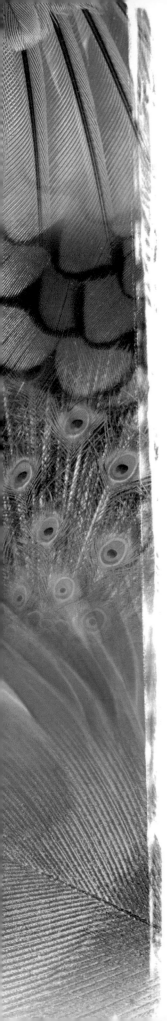

CONTENTS

This book looks at the orders of birds, their characteristics and the way each group of birds is adapted to its environment. Due to the number of orders, it is not possible to cover them all in this book. However, there is a complete list of the orders on page 44.

WHAT ARE BIRDS?

BIRDS ARE THE LARGEST AND FASTEST FLYING ANIMALS. Their ability to fly has meant that they have spread around the world and inhabit almost every type of habitat on land.

Bird features

Birds are a class of vertebrates. There are seven other classes of vertebrates, including mammals, reptiles and amphibians. All vertebrates have a vertebral column, which is a series of small bones running down their back to provide support. There are about 9,600 species of birds, which are divided into 27 orders.

All birds possess feathers and most species can fly. Their skeleton is adapted to flying, for example, the bones of the forelimbs support the wing. Their breastbone has an extension called a keel, which provides a strong anchor for the attachment of the flight muscles. Many bird bones are hollow, which makes their skeleton light and helps flight. Another feature of birds is the presence of a beak, which is formed from jawbones and covered by a tough sheath. Birds do not have teeth.

Birds are endothermic, or warm blooded, which means that their body temperature usually stays within a very narrow range, regardless of the outside temperature. This enables them to be active in cold environments, but it does mean that birds have to eat plenty of food to keep their bodies warm.

By changing the shape of its wings, this bald eagle (*Haliaeetus leucocephalus*) can increase or decrease the speed at which it flies.

CLASSIFICATION

About 2 million different organisms have been identified and sorted into groups, in a process called classification. Biologists look at the similarities and differences between organisms, and group together those with shared characteristics. The largest group is the kingdom, for example the animal kingdom. Each kingdom is divided into smaller groups, called phyla (singular phylum). Each phylum is divided into classes, which are divided into orders, then families, genera and finally species. A species is a single type of organism with unique features that are different from all other organisms, for example a golden eagle. Only members of the same species can reproduce with each other and produce fertile offspring.

The classification of a golden eagle (*Aquila chrysaetos*) is shown on the right.

| KINGDOM: Animalia |
| PHYLUM: Chordata |
| CLASS: Aves |
| ORDER: Falconiformes |
| FAMILY: Accipitridae |
| GENUS: Aquila |
| SPECIES: *chrysaetos* (golden eagle) |

One way of remembering the order of the different groups is to learn this phrase:
'**K**ings **P**lay **C**hess **O**n **F**ridays **G**enerally **S**peaking'.

Life cycle

Birds lay eggs with a hard shell. The eggs have to be kept at the right temperature in order for the chick inside to develop properly. Most birds build a nest and incubate their eggs until they hatch. Some chicks, such as those of blue tits and blackbirds, are born with no feathers and are completely dependent on their parents. They are called nidicolous chicks. Others, such as the chicks of ducks and geese, are born with feathers, and can feed themselves and run around within hours of hatching. They are called nidifugous chicks.

Adult blue tits (*Parus caeruleus*) make regular trips to the nest to feed their chicks.

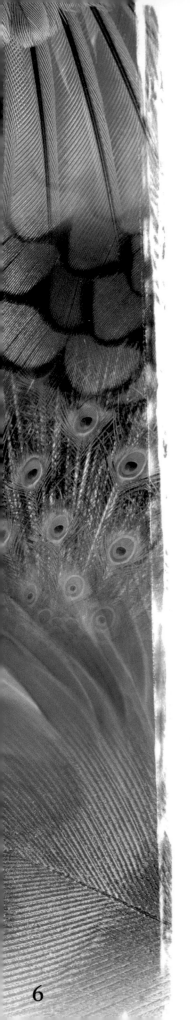

RATITES (STRUTHIONIFORMES)

OSTRICHES, RHEAS, CASSOWARIES, EMUS AND KIWIS belong to the order Struthioniformes. These birds have lost the ability to fly and are often called ratites. They are found mostly in the Southern Hemisphere.

Shared features

All ratites have a flat breastbone without a keel. The keel is essential for flight because it acts as a strong anchor for the wing muscles, so the lack of a keel means that ratites cannot fly. Their plumage is loose compared with other birds. Cassowaries and emus have feathers that hang down like hair. Each feather has two shafts of equal length. Ostriches, rheas and kiwis have shaggy-looking feathers with one shaft.

The African ostrich (*Struthio camelus*) is the largest living bird, reaching 3 m (10 ft) in height and weighing up to 135 kg (300 lb). Ostriches can run at speeds of 65 km/h (40 mph) to escape from predators such as lions and hyenas.

Ratites are running birds and their legs and feet are adapted for running. Most ratites are large birds with long, muscular legs that carry their body well above the ground. Unlike most other birds, which have four toes, most ratites have three. The ostrich is the only bird to have just two toes on each foot.

Eggs and incubation

Most ratites lay a large clutch of eggs. Often, several females lay their eggs in the same nest. As many as 12 female rheas lay their eggs in the same nest, so the clutch size may reach 60 or more. Unlike other birds, it is often the male ratite that incubates the eggs. The chicks are nidifugous, so they are able to leave the nest as soon as they have hatched and are cared for by the male.

Kiwis

Although the kiwi is included in this order, it is very different from its long-legged relatives. The kiwi is a small bird, about the size of a chicken, and it lacks tail feathers. It is a shy bird that is nocturnal (active at night). The kiwi is almost blind, but it has an acute sense of smell, which is generally rare in birds. It also has a highly sensitive beak.

Tinamous

The tinamou is another flightless bird that is sometimes included in the order Struthioniformes. It is a small, ground-living bird found in Central and South America. The tinamou is not completely flightless because it has small wings and can fly for short distances.

KEY CHARACTERISTICS
STRUTHIONIFORMES
- Flightless.
- Lack keel on breast bone.
- Loose feathers.
- Most have long legs with either two or three toes on each foot.

Cassowaries (*Cassuarius sp.*) live in the rainforests of Australia and New Guinea, where they search for fruits on the forest floor.

Penguins (Sphenisciformes)

Royal penguins (*Eudyptes schlegeli*) are found only on Macquarie Island, in the Pacific Ocean south of Australia. They share this island with the king, gentoo and rockhopper penguins.

Penguins are another group of flightless birds found in the Southern Hemisphere, particularly around the Antarctic and Southern Ocean. The order Spheniciformes contains 17 species of penguin, including the Adélie, emperor, king and rockhopper species.

Penguin features

The wings of a penguin are stiff, paddle-like and do not fold up at the sides of their bodies like other birds. Penguins use their wings to swim underwater. Their streamlined body slips easily through the water. Penguins have a very short, streamlined tail and their legs are well set back on their body so they can stand upright. Their three front toes are webbed.

Most penguins are adapted to life in cold habitats. They have a dense layer of short feathers and a layer of blubber (fat) under their skin to reduce heat loss. An unusual arrangement of blood vessels in their feet conserves body heat. Heat in the blood travelling towards the feet transfers into blood returning from the feet. This transfer of heat prevents heat being lost to the cold ice below the feet and allows the penguin to save essential body warmth.

Breeding on land

Penguins spend most of the year feeding at sea. However, they have to return to land to breed. Penguins return to traditional breeding places, called rookeries, where they live together in large groups, called colonies. Rookeries are mostly on the islands of the Southern Ocean, and along the coasts of Antarctica, southern Africa, the Galápagos islands, Australia and South America.

Extreme survival

Only two species of penguin can survive the extreme cold of the Antarctic winter. They are the emperor and Adélie penguins. Emperor penguins have an amazing life cycle. In April, at the beginning of the breeding season, the penguins walk inland to their rookeries. The female lays a single egg, which she passes to the male to incubate. The male incubates the egg on his feet, covered with a flap of skin. He stays on the ice through the dark, winter months while the female returns to the sea to feed. When the chick hatches, in the spring, the male gives it a meal regurgitated from his stomach. The female returns to take over the care of the chick and the male returns to the sea. By this time the males have lost much of their body fat and many do not survive the journey back to the sea. The chicks hatch with downy feathers that are not waterproof, so they must stay on the ice. The older chicks are left together in a crèche while both parents go to the sea to feed.

The young chicks of the emperor penguin (*Aptenodytes forsteri*) sit on the feet of their parents, under a flap of skin. The chicks will not have a complete set of feathers until they are six months old.

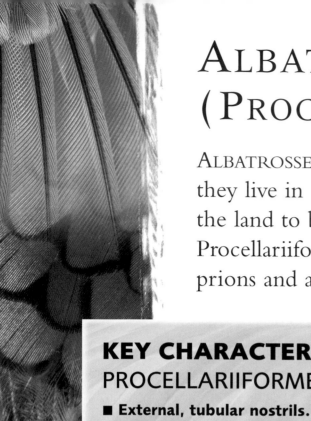

ALBATROSSES AND PETRELS (PROCELLARIIFORMES)

ALBATROSSES AND PETRELS ARE PELAGIC, WHICH MEANS they live in or over the open ocean. They only return to the land to breed. There are 92 species in the order Procellariiformes, including shearwaters, fulmars, petrels, prions and albatrosses.

KEY CHARACTERISTICS
PROCELLARIIFORMES

- External, tubular nostrils.
- Good sense of smell.
- Pelagic life, but breed on land.

Albatross features

The birds in this order have short tails and webbed feet with three toes. One distinctive feature is their long, external, tubular nostrils, which is why they are often referred to as 'tubenoses'. Their beak is straight, with deep grooves and a hooked tip.

Ocean life

Albatrosses and petrels fly continuously over the ocean, often for many months without returning to land. They even sleep while flying. They eat fish, squid and other marine animals that live in the surface waters. Albatrosses and petrels have to be able to drink sea water, so they have a salt gland beside each eye which filters out the salt from the water.

Excellent sense of smell

Albatrosses and petrels use their acute sense of smell to find food and locate their nest sites in the dark. It is thought that these birds also use smell to identify each other.

The razor-sharp, hooked beak of albatrosses, such as this wandering albatross (*Diomedea exulans*) is well-suited to catching fish.

PELICANS (PELECANIFORMES)

PELICANS AND THEIR RELATIVES ARE SEABIRDS. THE ORDER Pelecaniformes is made up of pelicans, gannets, boobies, cormorants, frigatebirds, darters, and tropicbirds. They are all strong fliers and swimmers.

KEY CHARACTERISTICS
PELECANIFORMES

- Totipalmate feet.
- Most have a large throat sac.
- Nostrils either small or sealed.

Pelican features

One unique feature of pelicans and their relatives is their feet. All four toes are joined together by a web. This arrangement is called totipalmate and it helps the birds to paddle when swimming. Most species have a large throat sac. Their nostrils are either small or sealed. The pelican has small nostrils that can be closed when diving. Gannets, cormorants and boobies have permanently sealed nostrils so they breathe through their mouths instead of their nostrils.

Life at sea

Pelicans and their relatives are adapted for life at sea. However, they have to come on to land to lay their eggs and most make use of cliffs, where they nest in large colonies. Their young are born completely helpless and rely on their parents for food. The birds in this order feed on fish and squid in the sea. They either dive into the water to catch fish, such as the gannet, or scoop fish up in their large throat pouches, such as the white pelican.

The white pelican (*Pelecanus erythrorhynchos*) has mostly white feathers with a long, flat, bright-orange beak and black-tipped wings. It feeds on fish, eating up to four large fish each day. When it catches a fish, the pelican tilts its beak up and swallows the fish whole.

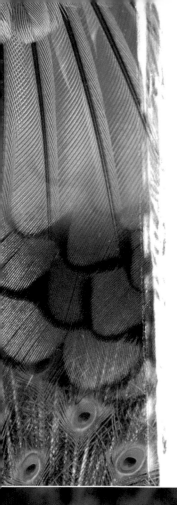

HERONS (CICONIIFORMES)

HERONS AND THEIR RELATIVES ARE FOUND AROUND THE world, along coastlines and near fresh water. They are not found in the northernmost parts of Alaska and Canada, Greenland, Antarctica, and some desert regions.

Classification

The order Ciconiiformes contains about 120 species, including herons, storks, egrets, ibises, spoonbills and bitterns. More recently, New World vultures such as the Californian condor and the turkey vulture have been included in this class too as a result of evidence from their DNA. New World vultures were previously classified with birds of prey.

Heron features

There is no unique feature that is common to all birds in this order. They are placed together because studies of their DNA show that they are related. However, many of the birds have relatively long legs and necks. Their necks have between 16 and 20 vertebrae, which gives them flexibility. Their bodies are relatively large and most have a spear-shaped beak. Although they spend a lot of time in water, the feet of these birds are not webbed. Instead, their four toes are widely spaced.

Herons such as this grey heron (*Ardea cinerea*) are expert hunters, using their long necks and beaks to catch fish in the water.

Habitat

Most herons and their relatives live near fresh water, although some can be seen in estuaries and along coasts. They feed mostly on fish, crustaceans, insects and carrion. They do not swim for food, but tend to stand motionless, watching for their prey to move before darting forward and stabbing it with their beak.

A number of these birds migrate in winter. They fly from their summer breeding grounds to warmer regions nearer the Equator, where they spend the winter before migrating back in the spring. The white stork, for example, spends the summer in southern Europe, where it nests on buildings, and winters in Africa. The migratory species of birds in this order are strong fliers with broad wings.

Herons

The heron is a typical example of this order. This is a wetland species, which wades in the shallows using its long legs to hold its body above the water. The heron hunts by standing still and watching, before darting forward to catch fish in its long beak. Herons have specialized feathers called powder down. These feathers are never moulted, but they fray from the tip and continually grow from the bottom. The fraying produces a fine powder that the birds use to clean their other feathers.

STORK NESTS

White storks have been building their nests on buildings across Europe and Asia since the Middle Ages. Their huge nests can be seen on rooftops, towers, chimneys, telephone poles, walls, haystacks and specially built nest towers. Some homeowners add wooden wagon wheels to old chimneys to encourage storks to nest on their houses.

White storks (*Ciconia ciconia*) build huge nests made of branches and sticks. The nests may be reused many times, with new material added each year. Some stork nests have been in continuous use for hundreds of years.

WATERFOWL AND SCREAMERS (ANSERIFORMES)

WATERFOWL ARE BIRDS WITH WATERPROOF FEATHERS that live on and beside water. They are common on wetlands, estuaries, ponds and lakes. They include ducks and geese, which were among the first birds to be domesticated and have been kept by people for thousands of years.

Waterfowl features

The order Anseriformes contains about 150 species divided into three families: ducks, geese and swans; screamers (named after their raucous, far-reaching cry); and magpie geese. These birds typically have a plump body with short legs. Their head is small relative to their body and their beak is broad and flattened. They are adapted for living on water, for example most have webbed feet for efficient swimming. The shape of their wings and their large webbed feet help them to take off from and land on water.

Feathers

All birds have to preen their feathers to keep them in good condition. They use their beak to clean and arrange the feathers. Most birds also smear oil over the feathers to keep them waterproof. The oil is produced by a preen gland,

Like many gamebirds (see pages 22–23), the male mallard (*Anas platyrhnchos*) is more colourful than the female. The mallard drake (male) has green and blue feathers while the female is a drab brown.

located near the base of the tail. In waterfowl and other aquatic species, the preen gland is better developed than in other birds.

Each year, waterfowl moult their feathers. Most species lose all their flight feathers at the same time so they are flightless for a period of about three to four weeks. However, the magpie goose loses its feathers gradually so it can still fly.

Life cycle

Swans build huge nests of leaves and twigs, but other species of waterfowl build simple nests using material they find around the nest site. Usually the female bird lines her nest with down feathers plucked from her breast. Ducklings and goslings are described as being nidifugous. This refers to the fact that they are born with downy feathers, are able to run around within hours of hatching and are soon able to follow their mother into water. This is essential because the young birds are vulnerable to attack from predators while they are on land.

The cygnets (young swans) of the mute swan (*Cygnus olor*) have grey, downy feathers. After two months, their white feathers start to appear and they can fly by the time they are four months old. Cygnets keep some of their grey feathers until after their first winter.

Feeding

Most waterfowl have a beak and tongue that are adapted to sucking food. Their fleshy tongue is covered in tiny spiny projections. The beak and tongue work together as a suction pump. Water is drawn in at the tip of the beak and expelled from the sides and back. Inside there are filters to trap small particles, which are licked off and swallowed.

Ducks have a wide beak that is ideal for dabbling in mud in search of small animals and for scooping up slugs and snails from grass. Geese have sharp-edged beaks, ideal for cutting blades of grass. The saw-billed ducks, such as fish-eating mergansers, do not suck up food. They have a beak that is long and hard with tooth-like serrations along the edge. This shape is perfect for catching slippery fish.

The greylag geese (*Anser anser*) spend the summer months in Iceland and northern Europe. At the beginning of winter, they migrate south to Scotland and other parts of Europe such as France and Spain.

Surviving the cold

Ducks and geese that live in the Arctic regions have to survive extremely cold weather, so they have an extra-thick layer of feathers and fat to provide essential insulation. Other species avoid the cold winters by migrating towards the Equator to warmer climates. For example, thousands of swans and ducks spend the summer months in the Arctic regions of Scandinavia, Iceland and Siberia, and the winter months further south in the east of England.

Communication

Waterfowl are vocal birds. They produce a range of sounds such as honks, hisses, quacks, trumpets and squeaks. Often the male has a different sound from the female. For example, the female mallard duck quacks while the male squeaks. The ruddy duck produces a drumming sound by beating its beak against its inflated throat sac.

Extra order: flamingos (Phoenicopteriformes)

The order Phoenicopteriformes contains six species of flamingos, four of which are found in the Americas and two in Europe and Africa. They live in large flocks near lakes and coasts. Flamingos are long-legged birds, 80–150 cm (31–60 in) in height with a slender body. Their long legs are adapted for wading in lakes and keeping their feathers out of the water. Flamingos feed on shellfish and algae. Their beaks are bent so that they can feed with their head upside down in the water. The inside of their beak is lined with rows of plates that are used to strain food from the water, while their thick tongue helps to suck in water.

Flamingo chicks have white feathers, but the adult feathers range in colour from light pink to deep red due to colour obtained from their food, especially shrimps.

FLAMINGO CHICKS

The larger species of flamingos build mound-shaped mud nests with concave tops. The female bird lays a single white egg into the nest, which hatches after about 30 days. Both the male and female flamingo produce a type of 'milk' from glands lining the upper part of their gut. They regurgitate and feed it to their chicks for about two months, until the chicks' beaks are developed enough to filter feed.

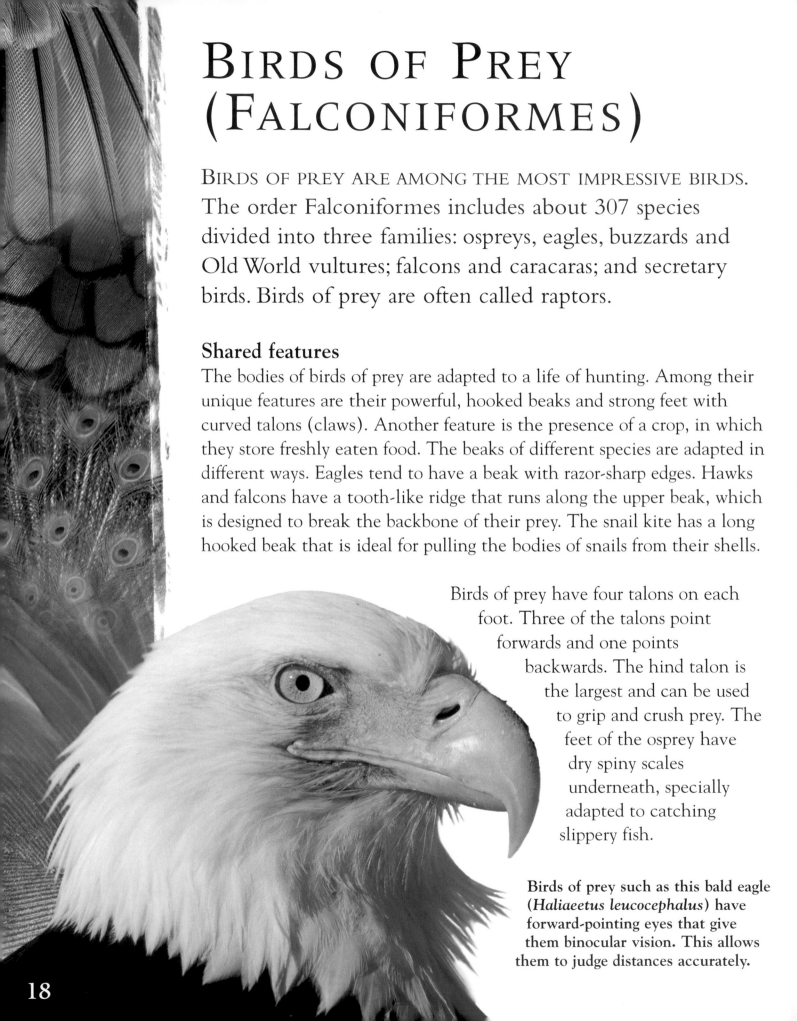

BIRDS OF PREY (FALCONIFORMES)

BIRDS OF PREY ARE AMONG THE MOST IMPRESSIVE BIRDS. The order Falconiformes includes about 307 species divided into three families: ospreys, eagles, buzzards and Old World vultures; falcons and caracaras; and secretary birds. Birds of prey are often called raptors.

Shared features

The bodies of birds of prey are adapted to a life of hunting. Among their unique features are their powerful, hooked beaks and strong feet with curved talons (claws). Another feature is the presence of a crop, in which they store freshly eaten food. The beaks of different species are adapted in different ways. Eagles tend to have a beak with razor-sharp edges. Hawks and falcons have a tooth-like ridge that runs along the upper beak, which is designed to break the backbone of their prey. The snail kite has a long hooked beak that is ideal for pulling the bodies of snails from their shells.

Birds of prey have four talons on each foot. Three of the talons point forwards and one points backwards. The hind talon is the largest and can be used to grip and crush prey. The feet of the osprey have dry spiny scales underneath, specially adapted to catching slippery fish.

Birds of prey such as this bald eagle (*Haliaeetus leucocephalus*) have forward-pointing eyes that give them binocular vision. This allows them to judge distances accurately.

Senses

Birds of prey have excellent eyesight and can see in far more detail than a human can. For example, they can spot a prey animal at a distance of several kilometres. This is due to the fact that they have large eyes that can collect a lot of light. There are also a large number of receptors, called cone cells, at the back of their eyes, which create a very detailed colour image when light falls on them. The eyes are protected and given shade by a ridge that lies over the eye sockets. Many of these birds have a nictitating membrane, or third eyelid, which gives further protection.

Life cycle

Most birds of prey have one partner and they may stay together for life, returning to the same nest each year. The nest is typically large, made of twigs and branches and set high up in trees, on tall buildings, or other vantage points. The female lays between one and three eggs, and the parents care for their young for several months until they are able to find food for themselves. Birds of prey are long-lived. They lay few eggs and their young take several years to reach maturity.

The female osprey (*Pandion haliaetus*) usually lays three to four eggs, one to two days apart. The chick that hatches first is more likely to survive if food is in short supply because it is larger than the other chicks and may even push them out of the nest. The young are ready to fly when they are about 55 days old.

Food and hunting

Almost all birds of prey are carnivorous and feed on a variety of prey animals, such as smaller birds, mammals, amphibians, reptiles, fish and even worms. They are superb predators that are adapted to catching prey with their feet and make good use of their excellent senses and strong flight. Most birds of prey hunt alone. Different species hunt at different times of the day, such as at dusk, dawn, or throughout the daylight hours.

Flight

Birds of prey spend much of their time in the air. They prefer to land on trees and other structures rather than walk on the ground. These birds are expert fliers. The larger species, such as vultures and large eagles, have long, broad wings for gliding. They make use of thermals (currents of rising warm air) to rise high in the sky, from where they can see prey a long way away. This is an energy-saving way of travelling since they hardly have to beat their wings. Falcons, which are small birds of prey, are so agile in flight that they

The osprey (*Pandion haliaetus*) eats mainly fish. When it spots prey, the osprey dives down and enters the water feet first, snatching the fish in its talons. Usually it takes off straight away, rearranging the fish in its talons on its way back to its perch so that the fish faces head-first and flying is smoother.

even attack other birds mid-air. Their wings tend to be narrower and more pointed, and they tuck them back to reduce their surface area and increase their speed when diving. Falcons usually swoop down on their prey from above. The expert is the peregrine falcon, which reaches speeds in excess of 200 km/h (124 mph). Birds such as the sparrowhawk and buzzard hover over the ground watching for small animals, before dropping down.

Scavengers

Some birds of prey, such as vultures and kites, scavenge for food. They have excellent eyesight and glide over the land looking for dead bodies on the ground. Different species of vultures tend to feed from different parts of a dead body. Some feed on the skin, while others eat the soft, fleshy parts of the body. Others plunge their heads deep into the carcass. These species usually have bald necks so their feathers are not covered in blood. The lammergeier is nicknamed the 'bone breaker' due to its habit of dropping large bones on to rocks to smash them and get at the bone marrow inside.

The secretary bird is different from other birds of prey. It spends most of its time on the ground, on long, stork-like legs. The secretary bird runs rather than flies after its prey, walking up to 24 km (15 miles) a day in search of food, which includes small mammals, lizards, snakes, and insects such as grasshoppers.

These Ruppells griffon vultures (*Gups ruppellii*) have gathered to feed on the carcass of a zebra that has been killed by lions.

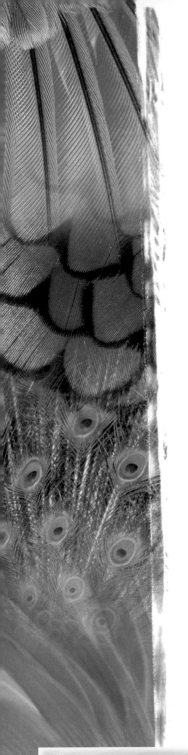

GAMEBIRDS (GALLIFORMES)

GAMEBIRDS ARE CHICKEN–LIKE BIRDS, MANY OF which have been domesticated and are eaten by people. They live in the wild around the world, apart from southernmost parts of South America and Antarctica.

The order Galliformes consists of about 280 species divided into seven families, including turkeys, jungle fowl (from which domestic chickens are derived), peacocks, grouse, ptarmigans and pheasants. These are mostly ground-living birds that often live in large groups. They vary in size from quails just 18 cm (7 in) long to peacocks that reach lengths of up to 2.3 m (7.5 ft).

Gamebird features
Typically, gamebirds have a plump body with a small head. Most have powerful flight muscles that provide a rapid take-off to escape from predators. Their beaks are short and thick, adapted for eating seeds or tough plant material such as heather shoots.

KEY CHARACTERISTICS
GALLIFORMES

- Birds have plump bodies and relatively small heads.
- Powerful flight muscles for rapid take off.

The male pheasant (*Phasianus colchicus*) has a distinctive fold of bright-red, fleshy skin hanging at the side of its head called a wattle, which stands out against the blue neck feathers.

Habitats and food

Gamebirds tend to live in ground that has plenty of cover, such as woodland edges and hedgerows. Most are herbivores, feeding on a variety of plant foods such as seeds, fruits and leaves. Some are omnivores, for example the turkey eats insects as well as seeds and roots.

Courtship

Many species of gamebird show distinct differences in appearance between the male and the female. This is called sexual dimorphism. The female tends to be smaller and drab in colour in contrast to the much larger male, who has brightly coloured feathers. The male peacock is famous for its spectacular train of feathers, which it fans out when courting. The peahen (female peacock) chooses a male by the size of his fan. Her offspring inherit the large fan size of the father, which has meant that peacock fans have become more colourful and larger over time. Male turkeys also have a tail fan and they make a gobbling call when courting. Capercaillies are noisy when courting, too. The males gather at a traditional breeding ground, called a lek, where they compete for females. The males strut around with their head up and tail feathers fanned out, making a loud noise a bit like a cork popping from a bottle.

When a male peacock (*Pavo cristatus*) raises his tail feathers during courtship, they form a fan. An adult peacock has an average of 200 tail feathers, which are shed and regrown every year.

Megapodes

Megapodes, such as the mallee fowl, belong to an unusual family of gamebirds. They are the only birds that do not incubate their eggs themselves. Megapodes lay their eggs under compost heaps made up of leaves. The eggs are incubated by heat generated from the rotting leaves. The birds push their beak into the heap to judge the temperature and regulate it by adding or removing leaves. After about 11 weeks, the young chicks hatch and have to dig themselves out of the nest.

OWLS (STRIGIFORMES)

OWLS ARE PREDATORY BIRDS BUT UNLIKE BIRDS OF PREY, they fly at night. They are found all over the world except in Antarctica, most of Greenland and some of the more remote Pacific islands.

The order Strigiformes contains approximately 213 species divided between two families. The family Tytonidae contains 18 species of barn owls. The family Strigidae, the typical owls, contains about 195 species, including the tawny and the snowy owl. Owls are solitary except while they are raising a family.

Barn owls (*Tyto alba*) may eat as many as 12 mice or voles a night if there is plenty of prey available. They often swallow their food whole, regurgitating the indigestible parts such as the bones and fur in the form of a pellet.

Owl features

Owls have a heart-shaped head with relatively large, forward-facing eyes, asymmetrically positioned ears and a hooked beak. They have a conspicuous circle of feathers around each eye, called the facial disc. Although owls have binocular (three-dimensional) vision, their large eyes are fixed in their sockets and they have to turn their entire heads around to change views. This is possible because their short neck is able to rotate. Owls have large ear openings, although unlike mammals, they do not have an external ear flap.

Hunting at night

Owls are mostly nocturnal and they show many adaptations to hunting in the dark, including excellent senses. They are far-sighted, which means they are unable to clearly see objects that are nearby but their long vision, particularly in low light, is excellent. This is because their large eyes trap all the available light.

Little owls (*Athene noctua*) nest in tree holes, walls, rabbit burrows and cliff holes. Only the male feeds the chicks at first, but the female helps later. After 26 days, the chicks leave the nest.

KEY CHARACTERISTICS
STRIGIFORMES

- Large, forward-facing eyes that are fixed in the sockets.
- Acute hearing.
- Hooked beak.
- Strong legs and feet with four sharp talons.

Many owls can hunt in total darkness using sound alone. Their facial disc helps to funnel the squeaks of prey such as rodents towards their ears. Their ears are widely spaced and placed asymmetrically. The time difference in sound reaching one ear before the other enables the owl to locate its prey precisely.

Catching prey

Owls catch their prey with their talons. They have a reversible outer toe, which changes position depending on whether they are gripping prey or perching. Owls mostly hunt small mammals, insects and other birds, although a few species specialize in catching fish. Their powerful talons and sharp beak enable them to tear their prey to pieces before eating. After swallowing, they regurgitate the inedible parts of their food as a pellet and spit it out.

CRANES, COOTS AND MOORHENS (GRUIFORMES)

GRUIFORMES IS A VARIED ORDER OF MOSTLY GROUND-living birds, found around the world apart from Antarctica. Many have an elaborate courtship involving vocal displays and dances. The order contains about 200 species of birds, divided between 12 families, including bustards, cranes, moorhens, crakes and rails.

Male great bustards (*Otis tarda*) compete with each other for females. They gather on display grounds, called leks, from where they try to impress the females.

Shared features

The appearance of the birds in Gruiformes is quite varied. Some are long-legged and look a bit like storks, whereas others are shorter and resemble gamebirds. However they all share one internal characteristic: they do not have a crop as part of their digestive system. Many of the cranes fly long distances, so they have long, broad wings. In contrast, some of the rails have small, rounded wings and fly poorly.

Adapted to habitat

Cranes and their relatives are well-adapted to their habitat. Bustards live in deserts and on grasslands, where there is little cover. They tend to be heavy birds and although they can fly, they rely on either running fast to escape predators or lying low. Their mottled brown plumage provides excellent camouflage.

KEY CHARACTERISTIC
GRUIFORMES
■ Absence of a crop.

Some of the waders, such as cranes and limpkins, have long, slender toes that help to spread their weight as they walk across muddy surfaces and prevent them from sinking in the mud. Cranes and limpkins share another characteristic – an extra-long windpipe that is so long that it is coiled in the chest. The length of their windpipe amplifies their call. The trumpeting call of a crane carries for many kilometres. Coots, rails and gallinules are found in wetlands around the world. They have partly webbed feet to help them swim.

Courtship

Some of the birds in this order have elaborate courtship displays, especially the cranes. Male and female cranes perform a dance that involves flapping their wings, jumping in the air and bowing to each other. Bustards, rails and bitterns also have a courtship dance. Cranes build a large nest in which they lay two eggs. Both parents help to incubate the eggs and raise the chicks. The young birds stay with their parents until the following breeding season.

Japanese cranes (*Grus japonensis*) carry out a spectacular and elaborate courtship dance in which the birds circle each other while leaping, calling and head-bobbing.

WADING BIRDS (CHARADRIIFORMES)

WADING BIRDS ARE FOUND NEAR SHALLOW WATER on coasts, lakes and rivers around the world. A few exceptions live in deserts and in thick forests. The order Charadriiformes contains about 340 birds divided into three suborders: waders, gulls and auks.

The avocet (*Recurvirostra avosetta*), a type of wading bird, has a distinctive, up-curved beak and long, slender legs that bend backwards.

Wading bird features

Waders have longish, slender legs, neck and beak. Most feed by probing into mud or picking food off the surface. Their long, narrow wings allow the birds to take off quickly. Gulls, skuas and terns are generally larger birds, with stouter legs and webbed feet for swimming. They take fish from the sea. Some gulls and skuas take food from beaches, and even rob smaller species of birds. Auks are coastal species that nest on cliffs and swim underwater to catch fish. They tend to have short legs, webbed feet and a plump body. They use their wings as flippers when they swim.

Beak and diet

Each bird's beak is adapted to its diet and the wading birds are no exception. The avocet has an up-curved beak which it sweeps through the water from side to side, immersing only the tip. Once it detects a small animal it darts forward to catch it. The curlew has a downward-curving beak for extracting animals buried deep in mud or sand. The oystercatcher has a bright-orange, probing beak, ideal for prising open mussels and oysters. The wrybill is the only bird with a beak that has a sideways curve, which it uses to flick stones aside when hunting for insects and other small animals.

Nesting

Many waders that live on the coast do not build a nest. They lay their eggs on shingle banks or on cliffs. Often the eggs are camouflaged so they are difficult to spot, for example the eggs of the little plover, which are laid amongst pebbles. A number of wading bird species, such as the guillemots, live and nest together in large colonies. Guillemots nest on cliff ledges, packed together very closely. The female guillemot lays a single, oval-shaped egg with a pointed end so that it rolls in a circle and not off the cliff. Each egg has a unique colouring, which the parents can identify when returning to a cliff ledge covered by eggs. Puffins dig a burrow up to a metre (3 ft) long to protect their eggs. They dig the burrow on clifftops and often line the nest inside with leaves or feathers. The female lays one egg at the end of the burrow, which is incubated by both parents.

The Atlantic puffin (*Fratercula arctica*) is easily identified by its flattened, brightly coloured beak, white face and black-ringed eyes. The puffin is an expert swimmer and may emerge from an underwater hunt with six or more small sand eels dangling from its beak.

Parrots (Psittaciformes)

Parrots are some of the most brightly coloured birds and many are kept as pets. They can be found in the wild in most warm parts of the world, including India, Southeast Asia and West Africa. The greatest number come from Australasia, South America and Central America.

Parrot features

The order Psittaciformes contains about 350 species. All the birds in this order have a characteristic curved beak and feet with four toes. Two of the toes face forwards and two face backwards, an arrangement referred to as zygodactyl feet. The arrangement of their toes helps parrots to grip branches and to hold fruit, nuts and other food. The beak is short and blunt, with a down-curved upper beak that fits over the smaller, lower beak. This beak shape is perfect for crushing seeds and nuts. Sometimes parrots use their strong beak to grip tree trunks as they climb. Their narrow, pointed wings provide agility and speed as they fly through the forests.

Parrots and cockatoos

The parrot order is divided into two large families: parrots, parakeets and lorikeets; and cockatoos. The term 'parrot' can be used to describe either the parrots and lorikeets family or the entire order. Parrots, parakeets and lorikeets are the larger family, with about 330 species. Parrots have an unusual texture to their

Macaws, such as this scarlet macaw (*Ara macao*), are a type of parrot, belonging to the parrots, parakeets and lorikeets family. They use their large, hooked beaks and their toes to grasp food such as fruit.

feathers, which scatters light to produce vibrant colours. Lorikeets have a brush-like tongue for collecting pollen and nectar, whereas parakeets and parrots have a broad tongue with a spoon-like tip for handling fruits and seeds. There are 20 species of cockatoos. They have a headcrest made up of stiff feathers that can be raised and lowered, and different skull bones from parrots and lorikeets.

Rainforest birds

Parrots live in large numbers in tropical rainforests. Their bright colours stand out against the mostly green foliage, which helps them to see each other. Parrots communicate using loud calls, which travel through the forest. Often they live in flocks, flying from tree to tree in search of food.

The kakapo

The kakapo is an odd-looking member of the parrot family that lives in New Zealand. It is the heaviest member of the order and is flightless. The kakapo is active at dusk, when it walks many kilometres each day in search of food. It chews plant leaves for their juice, leaving balls of chewed leaves hanging from plants. It also digs up roots.

The salmon-crested cockatoo (*Cacatua moluccensis*) comes from the Moluccan Islands in Indonesia. This cockatoo species is endangered because of habitat loss and from being trapped and sold as pets.

KEY CHARACTERISTICS
PSITTACIFORMES
- ■ **Zygodactyl feet.**
- ■ **Strong, curved beak.**

HUMMINGBIRDS AND SWIFTS (APODIFORMES)

HUMMINGBIRDS AND SWIFTS ARE SMALL BIRDS WITH AN amazing flying ability, found mostly in the warmer parts of the world. The order Apodiformes contains about 425 species divided into three orders: hummingbirds, tree swifts and swifts.

House swifts (**Apus affinis**) build saucer-shaped nests out of grass, pine needles, feathers, and even bits of paper or string, all glued together with mud and saliva.

Shared features

The word Apodiformes means 'unfooted birds', which refers to the weak legs and feet of these birds. Swifts are not able to perch. They use modified tail feathers to help them land and move on vertical surfaces. Both hummingbirds and swifts have a rapid wing beat and are acrobatic fliers. They can fly at speed and make sudden changes in direction.

Swifts

Swifts spend much of their lives on the wing (flying). Their narrow, sickle-shaped wings are well adapted for high-speed flight. All swifts are small birds, ranging in size from the pygmy swift, which weighs less than 6 g (0.2 oz) to the white-naped swifts at 200 g (7 oz). Swifts chase and catch their insect prey while flying. They can stay in the air all day, only returning to their roost at night. Eurasian swifts escape the cold winter weather by migrating to southern Africa, where it is warmer and there is more food. Male and female swifts look similar and both help with nest-building and rearing young. Many swifts nest in caves, on cliffs, or in hollows of dead trees. They often use saliva as glue to hold their nest together and to attach it to walls.

Hummingbirds

Hummingbirds are also small birds. They are best known for their beautiful, iridescent feathers and hovering flight. Most weigh less than 9 g (0.3 oz) and the smallest is a mere 2.5 g (0.09 oz). Hummingbirds feed mostly on nectar from flowers, although they also eat small insects. They are adapted to feed from flowers. To reach the nectar, hummingbirds have a narrow, elongated beak and a long tongue that ends in a brush tip to help sip the nectar. They have a hovering flight, in which their triangular wings beat in a figure of eight. They can hover, dart forwards and even fly backwards.

Hummingbirds' rapid flight and their high heart rate mean that they burn up a lot of energy, so they have to spend much of the day feeding. At night they go into a form of deep sleep called torpor in which their body temperature falls. While they are in torpor, the birds do not have to burn energy to keep warm. This is especially important for those hummingbirds that live at high altitudes, where night-time temperatures can fall below freezing.

The collared Inca hummingbird (*Coeligena torquata*) hovers in front of a flower as it inserts its long beak to reach the nectar deep inside. Hummingbirds are important pollinators for flowers because they transfer pollen from one flower to another as they feed.

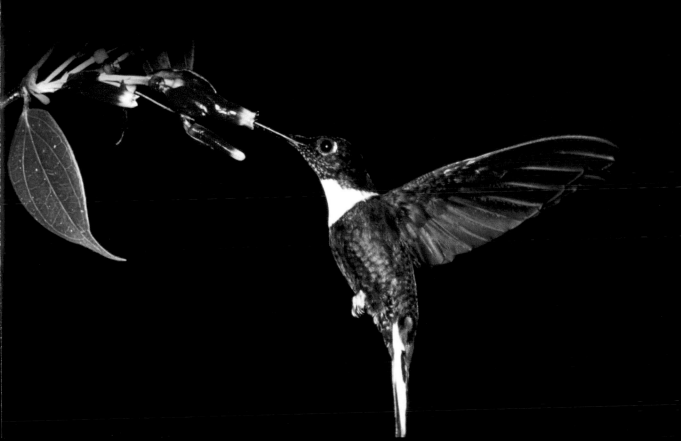

KINGFISHERS (CORACIIFORMES)

KINGFISHERS AND THEIR RELATIVES ARE OFTEN BRIGHTLY coloured birds. They have a widespread distribution, although most are found in Africa and Asia. There are just a few species in the Americas.

The order Coraciiformes is made up of about 190 species, divided into 10 families of very different appearance. They include the kingfisher, kookaburra, bee-eater hoopoes and hornbills.

Shared features

Most of the birds in this order have a large head with a prominent beak and a short neck. They have four toes, three of which face forwards. Their toes are often joined for part of their length. These birds lay white eggs in nests usually made in holes.

Hornbills

Hornbills are distinctive birds with a long, down-curved beak, which they use to feed, fight, preen and seal their nests. Many species have an unusual projection on the top of their beak called a casque. They also have long eyelashes. Hornbills have loud and very distinctive calls, especially the great Indian hornbill, which has a call like a roar. Researchers believe that the casque has a role in amplifying the call.

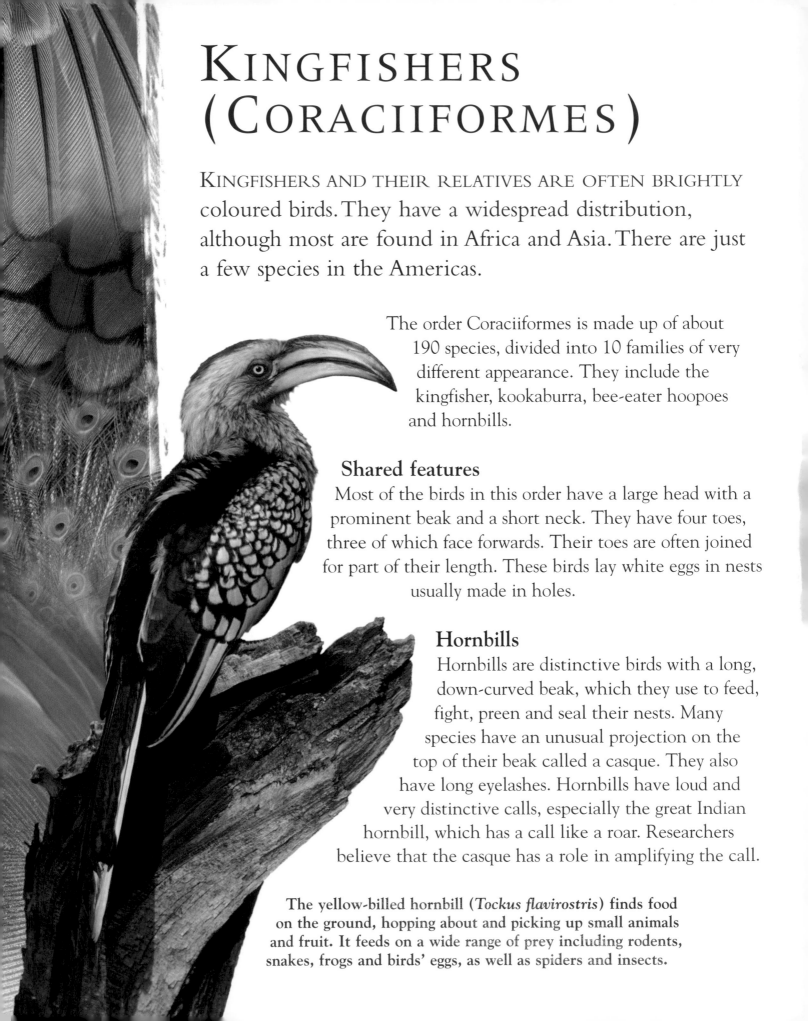

The yellow-billed hornbill (*Tockus flavirostris*) finds food on the ground, hopping about and picking up small animals and fruit. It feeds on a wide range of prey including rodents, snakes, frogs and birds' eggs, as well as spiders and insects.

Hornbills nest in holes in trees. They have a unique method of nesting. The male seals up the entrance to the hole while the female is inside, leaving a tiny slit. The female stays inside and incubates and then raises their young. The male passes her food through the slit.

Kingfishers

Kingfishers are usually brightly coloured birds with feathers in metallic blue, green and purple. They range in size from the pygmy kingfisher, which weighs about 10 g (0.4 oz) to the kookaburra from Australia, which is about 400 g (14 oz). Typically, kingfishers' beaks are long, straight and quite thick. However the beaks of fly-catching kingfishers are flattened from top to bottom, adapted to catching flies. They have short legs and short, rounded wings.

Kingfishers live mostly in wooded areas, often near water, and nest in holes made in riverbanks. The Eurasian kingfisher is an expert at fishing. It sits and waits for a fish to move and then dives down to catch it. It brings the fish back to its perch and kills it by striking it against a branch. Despite their name, not all kingfishers eat a diet of fish. Most species have varied diets that include insects.

The common kingfisher (*Alcedo atthis*) catches fish by diving beak-first into the water. It carries the fish back to its perch and beats it against the perch to kill it, before eating it head-first.

WOODPECKERS (PICIFORMES)

THE ORDER PICIFORMES CONTAINS ABOUT 380 SPECIES, divided into six families: woodpeckers, piculets and wrynecks; barbets; toucans; jacamars; puffbirds; and honeyguides. They are found all over the world apart from Australia and the polar regions.

Woodpecker features

All woodpeckers have zygodactyl feet, which are adapted to gripping tree trunks. Woodpeckers also have stiffened tail feathers, which are positioned to support the birds as they climb. Apart from the jacamars, the birds in this order never have any down feathers, at any age, only contour and flight feathers.

Nesting

Woodpeckers and their relatives nest in holes in trees. Typically they lay between two and nine white eggs. The young chicks are nidicolous (born without feathers), blind, and completely dependent on their parents.

Woodpeckers and barbets make their own nest holes, so they have a heavy beak for chiselling into wood. They also have a thickened skull to withstand the force of hammering and to act as a shock absorber. Honeyguides are different. Most honeyguides lay their eggs in the nests of other birds, such as woodpeckers and barbets. They usually only lay one egg in each nest, but the survival rate for their chicks is high because honeyguide chicks often kill all the other chicks in the nest using their hooked beak.

The male and female green woodpecker (*Picus viridis*) share the incubation of the eggs and both feed the young for about 19 days after they hatch.

Feeding

Most woodpeckers and their relatives are insectivores and feed on insects. They use their long tongues to pull out the insects that they find, often under bark. The green woodpecker has an exceptionally long tongue to reach deep into ant nests, catching them on the sticky tip. The acorn woodpecker is an omnivore, eating acorns as well as other seeds, fruits and insects. It has an unusual habit of storing acorns. It drills a small hole in the bark of a tree and pushes acorns firmly into the hole. Groups of up to ten related acorn woodpeckers work together to store acorns, often storing as many as 50,000 acorns in a single tree to last them through the winter.

Toucans eat mostly fruit, using their long beak to reach fruits on slender branches that would not support their weight. Once they have gripped the fruit in the tip of their beak, they toss their head to move the fruit into their throat.

Honeyguides were named after their habit of leading animals such as honey badgers to bees' nests. Once the animal has broken open the nest, the birds fly down to feed on the beeswax. Honeyguides also eat ants, termites, insect larvae and the eggs of other birds.

The toco toucan (*Ramphastos toco*) is the largest in the toucan family, with a colourful, long beak. The size of the beak means that the toucan cannot fly very well and spends much of its time in trees, hopping from branch to branch.

PERCHING BIRDS (PASSERIFORMES)

THE PERCHING BIRDS FORM THE LARGEST ORDER OF birds, with about 5,500 species – that's just over half of all the birds. Perching birds live in a wide range of habitats all around the world, apart from the Antarctic. They are most numerous in tropical regions.

The order Passeriformes includes birds such as the thrush, swallow, shrike, flycatcher, blackbird, finch, lyrebirds and ovenbirds. This huge order is divided into four suborders: broadbills and pittas, ovenbirds, tyrant flycatchers, and songbirds. Within these four suborders are about 80 families.

Perching bird features

The one feature common to all these birds is their perching feet. Perching birds have four toes, three of which point forwards and one that points backwards. They have an unusual arrangement of the tendons in their legs. When these birds land on a branch, their weight causes the tendons in their legs to tighten, which clamps the toes shut. This means that the feet grip the branch even when the birds are asleep.

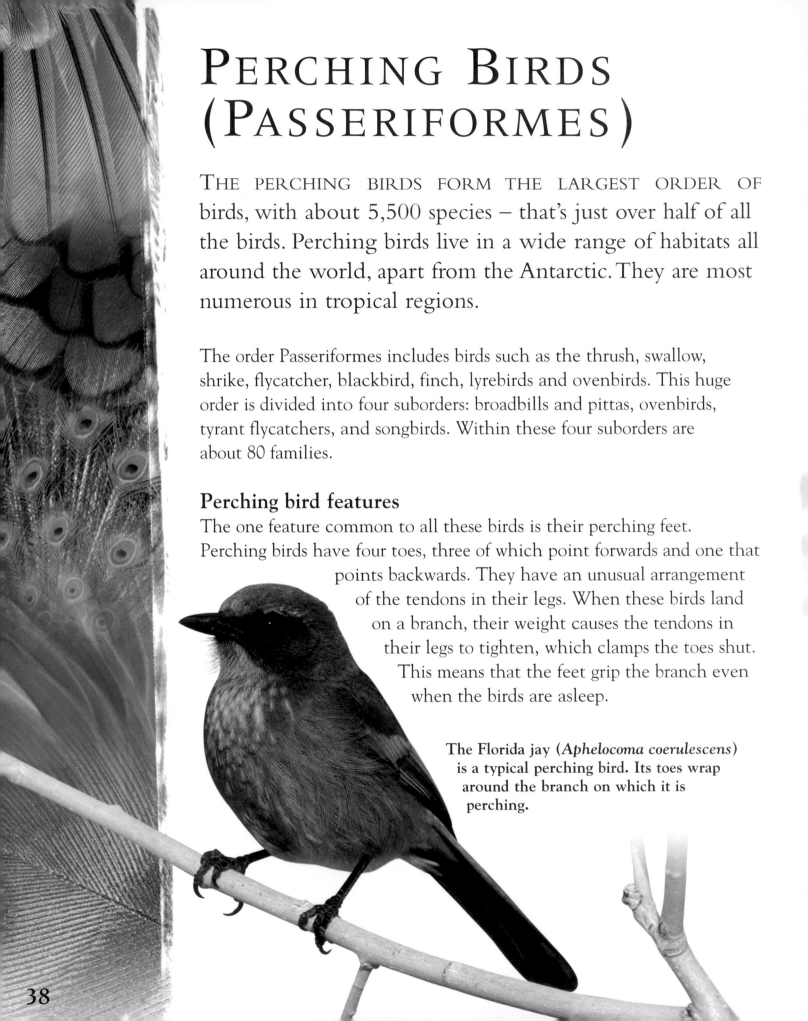

The Florida jay (*Aphelocoma coerulescens*) is a typical perching bird. Its toes wrap around the branch on which it is perching.

Songbirds

Many perching birds can sing. Birds have a type of voice box, or larynx, called a syrinx, which is located in the windpipe near the lungs. Membranes in the syrinx vibrate as air passes over them and this creates a sound. Muscles around the syrinx alter the sound. Songbirds have a particularly complicated syrinx which allows them to produce a much greater range of sounds than other birds. Each species of songbird has its own characteristic song. Some are incredibly beautiful, for example the song of the nightingale. Mostly it is the males that sing in order to attract a female and to protect their territory.

Bright colours

Perching birds include some of the most colourful of all birds, such as the bird of paradise from New Guinea and the bright orange cock of the rock from South America. Birds that live in tropical rainforests often have bright plumage, especially in reds and oranges. These colours stand out well against the green leaves of the trees and help the birds to see each other. In many species, the male is brightly coloured but the female has a drab plumage that is less noticeable to predators, especially when she is on the nest.

This male raggiana bird of paradise (*Paradisaea raggiana*) is performing a display that has attracted a female. The male spreads its wings, arches its back and raises its long plumes.

Food and habitat

Passerines (perching birds) are found in a wide variety of habitats, such as deserts, grasslands, woodlands, rainforests and gardens. Their diet varies depending on their habitat. Most species are small birds. To keep their body temperature at the right level and provide enough energy, they need to eat a lot of food every day. Many, such as robins and blue tits, eat high energy foods such as insects and seeds. Others, such as the sunbirds and honeyeaters, feed on nectar, which is rich in sugar.

Shrikes have a hooked beak with a tooth-like point at the end of the upper beak, which is ideal for gripping insects. Shrikes are nicknamed 'butcher birds' because of their habit of storing prey on thorns or barbed wire to eat later. The song thrush feeds on insects, worms and snails. It reaches the soft body of the snail by smashing the shell against a large stone, called an anvil. Swallows catch insects as they fly. In the winter, when insects are not available, swallows migrate to habitats with warmer climates.

Nest building

Passerines build some of the most elaborate nests in the bird world. The master builders are the weaver birds. These small, finch-like birds are found mostly in Africa. They weave their nests out of long strips of leaves, especially palm leaves. Their nests are roofed and often have long entrances, which protect the eggs and chicks from attack by predators such as snakes. Weavers build their nests beside others to make one huge structure on a tree. As many as 300 weaver birds may nest in the same tree.

This black-headed weaver bird (*Textor cucullatur*) has woven strips of leaves into a nest. The nest hangs from a branch, so it is difficult for predators such as snakes to get inside.

Bowerbirds are found in Australia, New Zealand and New Guinea. The male bowerbird builds a bower (arch) made from twigs and leaves. Once completed, he collects objects to decorate it. The blue bowerbird, for example, collects blue objects. Male bowerbirds use their bowers like a stage, to perform courtship displays in front of female bowerbirds. The females build nests in trees.

ANTING

All birds have to keep their feathers clean by preening. Jays have an unusual method – they use ants to clean their feathers! This is called anting. The jay disturbs an ant mound with its feet and allows the ants to climb over its feathers and spray their defence chemical of formic acid. The formic acid is thought to kill any parasites in the feathers.

This female satin bowerbird (*Ptilonorhynchus violaceusis*) is inspecting the bower made by a male (in front). The male has decorated the bower with blue and yellow objects such as feathers, pebbles, berries and shells. He struts around and sings while the female carries out her inspection. If she likes the bower, the birds will mate and she will fly away to build a nest nearby.

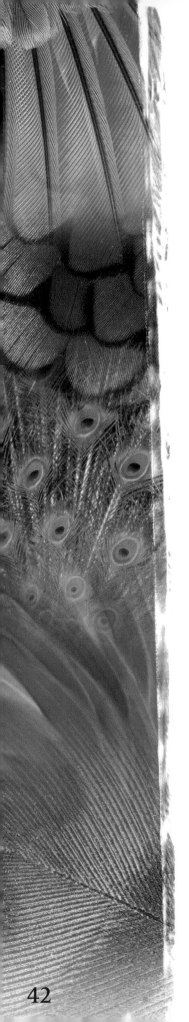

Under Threat

MORE THAN 1,000 SPECIES OF BIRDS ARE UNDER THREAT of extinction and many more are declining in numbers. The one order of birds that is under more threat than any other is the parrots. Parrots are attractive birds and many are caught and sold as pets, while others die when their habitat is destroyed.

Habitat loss

Virtually every habitat in the world, with the exception of urban habitats, has been damaged in some way. The most severely damaged are woodland habitats, which are important to birds because of the variety of nesting sites, roosting places and abundance of food. Rainforests, in particular, are home to a great number of bird species. Rainforests are being cleared at an ever-increasing rate, which is threatening species such as the hyacinth macaw, harpy eagle and bird of paradise.

Problems with farming

Farming has changed greatly over the last 60 years. In Europe, hedgerows and ponds have been cleared to make larger, more productive fields. In North America, prairie grassland has been ploughed up to make space for wheat. All these changes have destroyed important bird habitats.

Many barn owls (*Tyto alba*) on farms die after they have eaten the bodies of rats and mice that have been contaminated by rat poison.

These whooping crane chicks (*Grus americana*) have been bred in captivity. A researcher has dressed up in a whooping crane costume so the chicks will imprint on him. Whooping cranes migrate, but these young birds do not have any parents to follow. It is hoped that they will follow the researcher in the microlite as he leads them south to join other whooping cranes.

Farmers now use more chemicals, such as fertilizers and pesticides, than before. During the 1950s and 1960s, the pesticide DDT was sprayed on crops to kill insect pests. However this chemical did not break down easily in the environment and it affected birds when they ate the sprayed seeds. Birds of prey were even poisoned when they ate birds that had eaten the seeds. DDT in the birds of prey caused the females to lay thin-shelled eggs that broke easily in the nest. Today, traces of DDT can still be found in birds, even penguins, decades after the pesticide was used, and DDT is still being used in developing countries to control mosquitoes.

Conserving birds

There are many ways to protect and conserve birds. One is to protect their habitats. Another is by captive breeding, where a species is kept and bred in zoos or wildlife centres. If captive breeding is successful, some birds can be released back into the wild. The Hawaiian goose, or Ne Ne, was saved from extinction by captive breeding. A few birds were taken to Britain and bred in captivity successfully enough to release some back into the wild in Hawaii. Similar schemes have been set up to save the hyacinth macaw, Spix's macaw and the Californian condor.

PARROTS

More than 80 species of parrot are classed as endangered including the hyacinth macaw, which is the world's largest parrot, and the only flightless parrot, the kakapo. The Spix's macaw is the world's rarest bird. In the year 2000, the last known Spix's macaw in the wild disappeared. There are just 60 of these birds left in zoos and bird centres around the world.

BIRD CLASSIFICATION

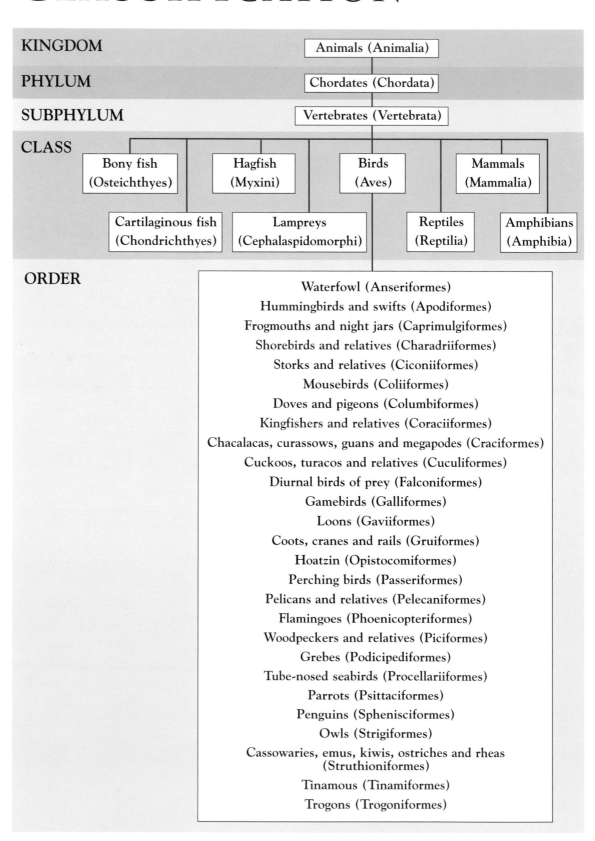

KINGDOM	Animals (Animalia)
PHYLUM	Chordates (Chordata)
SUBPHYLUM	Vertebrates (Vertebrata)

CLASS

| Bony fish (Osteichthyes) | Hagfish (Myxini) | Birds (Aves) | Mammals (Mammalia) |

| Cartilaginous fish (Chondrichthyes) | Lampreys (Cephalaspidomorphi) | Reptiles (Reptilia) | Amphibians (Amphibia) |

ORDER

Waterfowl (Anseriformes)
Hummingbirds and swifts (Apodiformes)
Frogmouths and night jars (Caprimulgiformes)
Shorebirds and relatives (Charadriiformes)
Storks and relatives (Ciconiiformes)
Mousebirds (Coliiformes)
Doves and pigeons (Columbiformes)
Kingfishers and relatives (Coraciiformes)
Chacalacas, curassows, guans and megapodes (Craciformes)
Cuckoos, turacos and relatives (Cuculiformes)
Diurnal birds of prey (Falconiformes)
Gamebirds (Galliformes)
Loons (Gaviiformes)
Coots, cranes and rails (Gruiformes)
Hoatzin (Opistocomiformes)
Perching birds (Passeriformes)
Pelicans and relatives (Pelecaniformes)
Flamingoes (Phoenicopteriformes)
Woodpeckers and relatives (Piciformes)
Grebes (Podicipediformes)
Tube-nosed seabirds (Procellariiformes)
Parrots (Psittaciformes)
Penguins (Sphenisciformes)
Owls (Strigiformes)
Cassowaries, emus, kiwis, ostriches and rheas (Struthioniformes)
Tinamous (Tinamiformes)
Trogons (Trogoniformes)

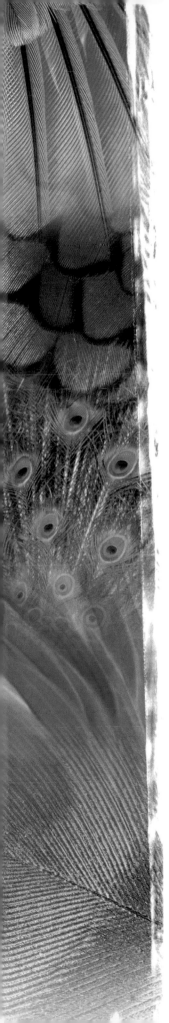

GLOSSARY

adapt To change over time in order to cope with the environment.

algae Aquatic, plant-like organisms that range in size from simple single-celled plankton to large seaweeds.

asymmetric Not symmetric. Of owls' ears, placed at different heights on either side of the head.

binocular vision A type of vision that uses two eyes facing forwards to produce a three-dimensional image.

breeding season A period of the year when mating and egg-laying take place.

camouflage Colours and patterns that let an animal blend in with its background.

carnivorous An animal that hunts and eats other animals.

carrion Dead or decaying flesh.

casque A helmet-like structure on the head of birds such as the hornbill.

classification The way in which animals and plants are placed in different groups.

clutch A set of eggs, usually laid by one bird and incubated at the same time.

colony A large group of birds that breed in the same area.

compost A substance made of rotting plant and animal material that is added to soil to increase its nutrient content.

courtship A type of behaviour before mating.

crop A sac at the bottom of a bird's oesophagus, in which food can be stored.

crustacean An animal that has a heavy exoskeleton and jointed legs, for example a crab, lobster or prawn.

domesticated Tamed and kept by people for food or as pets.

downy feathers Small, soft feathers that lie close to the skin of a bird, trapping heat.

endothermic Having a high body temperature that is kept within a narrow range, regardless of the temperature of the surroundings.

estuary The mouth of a river where it enters the sea.

extinction No longer living.

gland A group of cells that work together and produce a secretion, for example the salivary glands produce saliva in the mouth.

imprint To recognize and become attached to the parent, or an object that is pretending to be the parent.

incubate To keep eggs at the right temperature for chick development. Incubation is usually carried out by the parent birds.

insulation A way of keeping either warm or cool, to control the temperature.

keel An extension along the breastbone of a bird for the attachment of flight muscles.

migrate To make a regular journey between two different places at certain times of the year.

moult The annual shedding of feathers, quickly followed by the growth of new feathers.

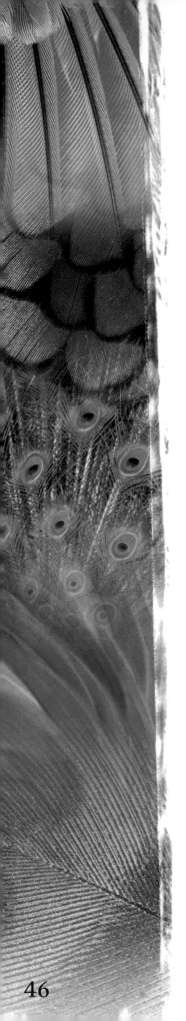

GLOSSARY

nictitating membrane A thin membrane that moves sideways across the eye; also called the third eyelid.

nidicolous A newly hatched bird that is blind, naked and completely helpless at birth.

nidifugous A chick that is born with a covering of down feathers and open eyes, and can run around and feed within minutes of hatching.

nocturnal Active at night.

oesophagus The tube that runs from the mouth to the stomach.

omnivore An animal that eats both plant and animal foods.

order A category of organisms in the system of classification, ranking above a family and below a class.

parasite An organism that lives on or in another organism, causing that organism harm, for example fleas and tapeworms.

pelagic Living in or over the ocean.

plumage Birds' feathers.

predator An animal that hunts other animals for food.

preening Cleaning the feathers.

prey Animals that are hunted and eaten for food by other animals.

raptor Another name for a bird of prey.

regurgitate To bring the contents of the stomach back into the mouth.

rookery The breeding place of birds such as penguins and rooks.

scavenge To feed on the remains of dead animals.

sexual dimorphism Male and female birds that have a different appearance, for example the male and female ostrich and mallard.

shaft The central 'stem' of a feather, which is hollow.

shingle banks Banks at the top of a beach, above the high-tide mark, formed from stones and gravel pushed up the beach by the tide.

sp. An abbreviation for 'species', used in the Latin names for animals where the exact species is unknown.

species A group of individuals that share many characteristics and can interbreed to produce fertile offspring.

streamlined Having a sleek, tapering shape that moves through the air or water easily.

syrinx The vocal organ of a bird.

talons Strong, curved claws of a bird such as a bird of prey or owl.

tendons The tough bands that join muscle to bone.

thermals Warm air currents that enable some birds to glide effortlessly through the air.

tropical Relating to the hot regions of the world, between the tropic of Cancer and the tropic of Capricorn.

waterfowl Birds that live on or near water, for example geese and ducks.

webbed Having skin connecting the toes, which is helpful for swimming.

zygodactyl Having feet with the first and fourth toes directed backwards and the second and third toes pointing forwards.

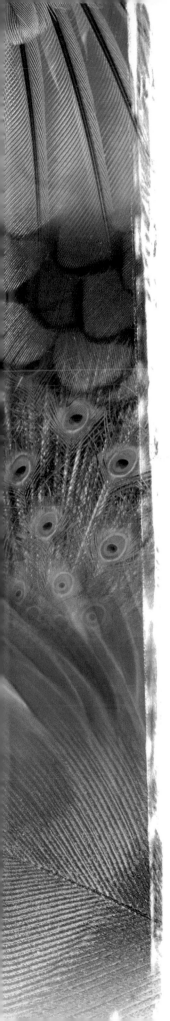

FURTHER INFORMATION

Books

100 Things You Should Know About: Birds by Jinny Johnson (Miles Kelly Publishing, 2004)

21st Century Debates: Endangered Species by Malcolm Penny (Hodder Wayland, 2003)

Animal Classification by Polly Goodman (Hodder Wayland, 2004)

Animal Kingdom: Birds by Sally Morgan (Raintree, 2004)

Classifying Living Things: Classifying Birds by Andrew Solway (Heinemann Library, 2003)

DK Animal Encyclopedia (Dorling Kindersley, 2000)

The Encyclopedia of Animals: Mammals, Birds, Reptiles, Amphibians editors Forshaw, Gould and McKay (Fog City Press, 2002)

Encyclopedia of Birds editor Christopher Perrins (Firefly, 2003)

Life of Birds by David Attenborough (BBC Worldwide Publishing, 1998)

Life Processes series: *Classification* by Holly Wallace (Heinemann Library, 2002)

Living Nature: Birds by Angela Royston (Chrysalis Children's Books, 2003)

Nature Files series: *Animal Groupings* by Anita Ganeri (Heinemann Library, 2003)

Science Answers: Classification by Richard & Louise A. Spilsbury (Heinemann Library, 2004)

Visual Encyclopedia of Animals by Barbara Taylor (Dorling Kindersley, 2000)

Websites

The Animal Diversity Web
http://animaldiversity.ummz.umich.edu
A huge site covering all the animal groups, compiled by the staff and students at the Museum of Zoology, University of Michigan.

BBC Nature
http://www.bbc.co.uk/nature/animals/birds/
Webcams, birdsong recordings, species facts and suggestions for things to do to encourage wild birds into gardens.

Bird Families of the World
http://montereybay.com/creagrus/list.html
Website providing information on all the families of birds with text and photos.

National Audubon Society
http://www.audubon.org/
A leading organization in the USA concerned with the conservation of birds. The website features webcams of nesting birds, information sheets, news items and results of bird counts.

RSPB
http://www.rspb.org.uk
Organisation that promotes the conservation of birds. The website includes an A-Z of UK birds, webcams, surveys and news about issues concerning wild birds.

Wildfowl and Wetlands Trust
http://www.wwt.org.uk/
UK conservation organization concerned with the protection of wildfowl and wetland habitats. Lots of information on wildfowl, including swans, geese and ducks.

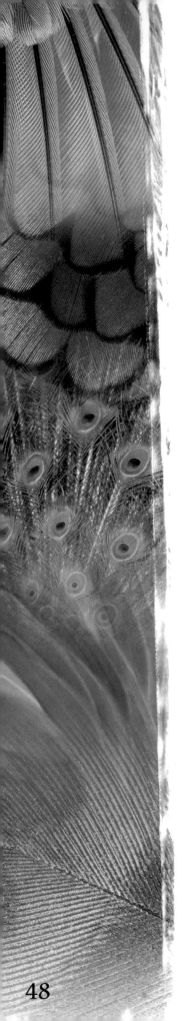

INDEX

Page numbers in bold refer to a photograph or illustration.